HOLT AND DISTRICT

A Portrait in Old Picture Postcards

by

Rhoda Bunn

S. B. Publications
1990

For my family.

First published in 1990 by S. B. Publications
19 Grove Road, Seaford, East Sussex, BN25 1TP

Reprinted 2000

Typeset and printed by Geo. R. Reeve Ltd., Wymondham, Norfolk NR18 0BD.

CONTENTS

Acknowledgements v

Introduction . . . . vi–vii

The Holt Crest viii

A multi-view postcard of Holt 1

Spout Hills 2

The Obelisk and High Street 3

New Street 4

Mr. Ben Empson, New Street 5

The Windmill 6

Rounce and Wortley's Printing Works 7

The Water-Tower, Shirehall Plain 8

Byford's Fire 9

Market Place 10

Chapman's Bakery, Fish Hill 11

Market Place and Church Street 12–13

Old School House and 'Blind Sam' 14

St. Andrew's Church 15

White Lion Street 16

Cook's Stage-coach at the 'White Lion' 17

Post Office Corner 18

Cromer Road 19–22

Holt Hall 23

Gresham's School 24

'Woodlands', Cromer Road 25

Home Place 26

Flood Damage, Hempstead Road 27

Donkey Express 28

CONTENTS CONTINUED

The Lows 29
Holt Railway Station 30–31
Market Place 32
High Street 33–35
Beating the Bounds 36
Hunworth 37
Stody Lodge 38
Briston 39–40
Edgefield 41–43
Corpusty Station 44
Matlask 45
Hempstead 46–47
Baconsthorpe 48–49
Erpingham 50–51
Kelling 52–55
Weybourne 56–57
Langham 58–59
Saxlingham Floods, 1912 60
Glandford 61–63
Bayfield 64–65
Letheringsett 66–68
Bale 69
Gunthorpe 70
The Preston Brothers 71
Just 'A Line' from Holt 72

S.B. Publications

Abbreviations used in text. c – circa; p.u. postally used.

ACKNOWLEDGEMENTS

My grateful thanks are due to Archie Checkley for all his help with facts gleaned from his vast knowledge of Holt and the surrounding area, and to Philip Standley for his help and advice on this, my first venture into print.

Not forgetting my daughters, Jane for typing and Chris for additional typing, without whom this book would not have been possible.

Margaret Scoble for editing.
Steve Benz for final editing and marketing.

For the loan of various postcards:

Archie Checkley; pages 5, 14, 18, 21, 37, 41, 45, 46, 48, 54, 63, 64, 66, 67, 68, 69, 71 and 72.

Philip Standley; pages 6 and 58.

INTRODUCTION

The name of Holt is derived from the Saxon word meaning wood. It is thought that the name comes from the fact that there was much afforestation in the area to alleviate the cruel winds from the sea. There are no records of Holt before it was mentioned in the Domesday Book, where it is described as one of the manors held by Edward the Confessor, and then by William I after the Norman invasion. Holt had five of the five hundred and eighty water-mills in Norfolk in 1086, and its own port, thought to be Cley; a separate hamlet attached to the Manor of Holt. Also attached to the Manor were Blakeney, Bale, Hempstead and parts of Briston and Sharrington. Holt had its own market, and by the time it was closed in the 1960s, the market had existed for almost a thousand years. As a Norfolk country acquaintance would say: "Thass bin thear a rear long time".

During the reign of Queen Elizabeth I (1558–1603), Holt's population was less than five hundred. In 1592, there came "a great plage which beganne 4th Auguste continewed unto ye 26 of Ffeb followinge". The "plage" was probably typhoid, due to the absence of any sanitation, and in those seven months, sixty-four people died. Edmund Cooke buried his wife and six children within twelve days, James Leman lost three children and he was buried along with the fourth and Andrew Estmes buried a daughter on September 20th, a son on the 23rd, and was laid, ten days later in one grave with his wife and another son and daughter, followed by his last little girl within a week. Such were the sorrows of those times.

In 1708, a terrible fire occurred which considerably altered the face of the town. Starting near the Shirehall Plain, the fire was said to have spread with such rapidity that the butchers did not even have time to rescue meat from their stalls. After the fire, the town received generous donations from all over the county: North Walsham sent £32.12.6d., and Hingham £10.13s – considerable sums in those days. Gradually, the town was rebuilt, replacing the large number of properties destroyed, leaving a legacy of many fine Georgian buildings many of which survive today.

Holt's population continued to grow and by 1801, there were two hundred and twelve houses with 1,004 inhabitants, rising to 1,726 in 1851. The latter half of the nineteenth century saw a decline in the population. This was probably caused by emigration to the colonies, as records reveal that many local people applied for assisted passage to Australia and Canada where gold had been discovered.

By the beginning of the twentieth century, the decline in population had been reversed and the market town grew steadily. Today, Holt has become a busy town serving a wide area and offers an excellent centre for tourists to explore the many attractions of the North Norfolk coastline and surrounding countryside.

This book provides a nostalgic tour of the town and its surrounding villages illustrated by old and rare picture postcards. Old postcards are now recognised as a valuable record of life in times past, and we have much to thank the early photographers who faithfully recorded the towns, villages and their inhabitants in so much detail. The majority of the postcards reproduced in this book have been selected from my own collection, assembled over the last ten years, and I believe that some of the cards have not been seen since their original publication approximately eighty years ago.

My family connections with the area go back many years. I was born at Briston, near Holt, spending my early years there, and educated at Miss Eva Preston's Orchard Preparatory School in Hempstead Road, Holt in the 1930s: one of my earliest recollections being a journey in my grandmother's pony and trap when delivering grapes to Bond's fruiterers on Fish Hill, Holt. Although I have lived in Wymondham for the last forty years, I have returned frequently to Holt visiting family and friends, and have always retained my affection for the area. I trust this book will give many hours of pleasure to older and younger residents alike and give an insight into the way of life all those years ago.

Rhoda Bunn
Wymondham
April 1990

In preparation by the same author: Melton Constable and District

THE HOLT CREST

The crest appears to be a combination of the crests of the Gresham family, Gresham's School and the Worshipful Company of Fishmongers who were appointed governors when Gresham's School opened and still remain as trustees of the school. It consists of a merman and mermaid each side of a shield. The upper part of the shield consists of three crossed keys on a red background, two sets of crossed fishes on a blue background below, with three fishes in between. The motto is the same as the Company of Fishmongers: "All worship be to God only".

A MULTI-VIEW POSTCARD OF HOLT, p.u. 1908

This novelty postcard incoporates five different views of the town centre: the church, the windmill, Letheringsett Road, and several pictures of the surrounding countryside. It also depicts the town mascot – an owl – in the full stop.
(Published by Preston Bros., Holt)

2957. SPOUT HILLS, HOLT.

SPOUT HILLS, c. 1924

Spout Hills was one of two commons allocated to the poor of the town in the 1810 Enclosures. The spring water to be found here is noted for its clarity. The pumping station situated by the Letheringsett Road pumped water to the water-tower on Shirehall Plain (see page 8). Peeres (or Peres) wood can be seen in the left background, and Burrough's Windmill on the skyline (see page 6).

('Sepia Series' postcard produced for Starlings, The Library, Market Place, Holt.)

HOLT OBELISK & HIGH STREET

THE OBELISK AND HIGH STREET, p.u. 1914

Holt's stone obelisk, with its pineapple finial and mileages to various places carved on its sides, is said to be one of a pair which once supported the gates to Melton Constable Park. The second obelisk stood in East Dereham Market Place until it was demolished in 1919 to make way for the War Memorial. Looking in an easterly direction along High Street and showing, in the left foreground, the premises occupied at the time by Mr. Walter Horne, a monumental mason; notice the stone slabs stacked against the wall. On the right is Roundways House, a listed building which was once a doctor's surgery.

NEW STREET, c. 1926

Looking towards High Street and showing the Old Board School on the left. Built in 1851, at a cost of £600, the old Board School was first known as the British School, and later as the Council School. It closed in October 1928 when the New Holt School opened in Norwich Road. Messrs. Dyson and Faircloth's Garage now stands on the site of the old school building. The Queen Adelaide public house can be seen further down New Street on the right.

MR. BEN EMPSON, NEW STREET, c. 1912

Mr. Ben Empson photographed outside his home in New Street, ready to depart on a trip in this smart two-in-hand carriage. Mr. Empson owned the local riding school, and kept horses and various carriages for hire. The family also had a bakery, run by Mr. Joseph Empson. A board advertising Daren Bread can be seen on the wall behind Mr. Empson.
(A.P. Checkley collection.)

THE WINDMILL, p.u. 1908

Holt's windmill was built in 1795. It was powered by wind and steam and situated on the corner of Mill and New Streets. The miller at the time was Mr. Sidney Burroughes who also owned the mill. As well as being a corn, hay and chaff merchant, he sold coal and coke, and provided his services as a carting contractor, with a depot at the Railway Station. The mill ceased working in 1925 and at present the site is occupied by a cash and carry warehouse.

(Philip Standley collection.)

ROUNCE AND WORTLEY'S PRINTING WORKS, c. 1910

A Cromer firm, Messrs. Rounce and Wortley took over Arthur Preston's 'Reliance' Printing Works in 1908. This picture shows the staff assembled outside the printing works in the High Street. When the business closed, the building was demolished, and the vacant site became Rust's Food Market. The double-fronted shop, centre background, was occupied by F.W. Baker, grocer and draper. On the right, part of the Manor House can be seen.

No. 4 Dack Series

Holt. Water Tower, Shirehall Plain.

THE WATER-TOWER, SHIREHALL PLAIN, p.u. 1905

The water-tower was erected in 1885 on Shirehall Plain by Erpingham Rural Sanitary Authority. The 56ft-high tower held 15,000 gallons of water which was pumped up from Spout Hills (see page 2). Water-carts from outside the town, still continued to bring freshwater to the town and sold it for a farthing per pail; even after the water-tower was in operation. In the background are the extensive ironmonger's premises of Henry Byford, and to the right of the picture, the Shirehall building that held the County Court Sessions.

(This postcard was produced by Photoplane Co. for Mr. Dack, who was engagingly described in one directory as 'Tobacconist and Birdstuffer, Cromer Road'.)

BYFORD'S FIRE, 1906

Henry Byford's premises on Shirehall Plain suffered serious damage when fire broke out during the night of 18th November 1906. With the fire engine stationed only yards away, firemen were quickly at the scene and the nearby water-tower provided plenty of water to contain the blaze. A newspaper report on the event states that although the shop's stock of gunpowder exploded in the flames, the firemen managed to prevent the stock of cartridges doing the same. The shop was rebuilt and continued trading until 1986.

(Published by Preston Bros., Holt.)

PRINTED AT ARTHUR PRESTON'S "RELIANCE" WORKS, HOLT.

MARKET PLACE, HOLT.

MARKET PLACE, p.u. 1905

On the right is Elden House which later became a branch of Lloyds Bank. Neal's, cycle agent and repairer, is on the left of the picture, and Gresham's Old School House can be seen in the distance. This postcard was printed by Arthur Preston who was an industrious businessman. Besides owning the printing works, he ran the Concert Hall in New Street, sold and hired out musical instruments, gave music lessons, and was also the organist at Holt Church.

CHAPMAN'S BAKERY, FISH HILL, c. 1906

Mr. Joseph Chapman's Bakery on Fish Hill, with the owner and staff posing outside. Notice the ladder used to carry the heavy sacks of flour to the store on the first floor – a back-breaking job. By 1912 a Miss Annie Chapman was the proprietor of the Bakery. Today the premises are divided into two shops, one of which is a hairdressing salon.
(Published by Preston Bros.)

MARKET PLACE AND CHURCH STREET, c. 1907

Preston Brothers were photographers, newsagents, picture framers and published their own postcards. Their shop was situated in Market Place before they moved their business to New Street in 1914. The church tower can just be seen on the skyline. Before Holt's disastrous fire, the church had a steeple which was said to have been used as a seamark by shipping.
(Published by Preston Bros.)

MARKET PLACE, 1921

The War Memorial was dedicated and unveiled on the 29th May, 1921 – the day this picture was taken. The postcard also shows the front entrance to Holt's cinema. Although there had been film-shows at various venues before, this was Holt's first "permanent" cinema, opening 2 or 3 nights per week in a corrugated-iron building at the rear of the large house on the left. On rainy nights, customers would move their seats to avoid drips from the roof! The proprietors also had a mobile projector which was taken to Briston by car for showing films there on Thursday and Friday nights. The cinema moved to the Co-op Hall in New Street about 1930 and closed in 1937, when the Regal was built in Peacock Lane.

OLD SCHOOL HOUSE AND "BLIND SAM", c. 1907

Sir John Gresham converted the Manor House into a Grammar School which opened in 1562. Sadly, Sir John died of the plague before the school opened. The original School House was pulled down in the late 1850s and the postcard shows the new building, which opened in c. 1860. In front of the School House is the illuminated fountain erected in 1887 to celebrate Queen Victoria's Diamond Jubilee. It was affectionately known by local folk as "Blind Sam" because it was seldom lit. In this picture, children can be seen drinking from the fountain. In 1921 it was removed to Obelisk Plain to make way for Holt's War Memorial.

(A.P. Checkley collection)

ST. ANDREW'S CHURCH, p.u. 1907

St. Andrew's Church is built in the Decorated and Perpendicular styles, with the register dating from 1558. It suffered grievous damage from the town's fire in 1708, when sparks set light to the then thatched chancel. The heat was so intense that it melted the lead on the roof which ran down the walls causing serious cracks. The tall steeple also caught fire and collapsed, bringing the bells crashing to the ground. Repairs and restorations were made during the early nineteenth century, and in 1882 the organ was built at a cost of around £500.

WHITE LION STREET, c. 1907

White Lion Street is situated at the east end of the Market Place. Behind the wall, to the left of the White Lion Hotel, was a Quaker Burial Ground and some cottages which were demolished in the 1930s to make way for Holt's present Post Office. The white house adjoining the White Lion, in the centre background, is 'Wansbeck House' which was occupied in the early 1800s by a surgeon, John Banks who thought so much of his horse that he had a memorial stone put in the churchyard wall when the horse died. Today Baldry's Refreshment Rooms are now occupied by Martin's Newsagents and shops have been built to the right of the White Lion Hotel.

COOK'S STAGE-COACH AT THE 'WHITE LION', c. 1907

Cook's Stage-coach outside the White Lion Hotel. It must have been a special occasion as the usual route for Cook's Stage-coach was from 'The Maid's Head' at Norwich, to Cromer via Aylsham and Roughton. This coach was generally known as the "Lobster" Coach and was drawn by five horses. On the left, notice the sign for the 'Angel Inn' which ceased trading around the time the new Post Office was built.

The White Lion Hotel Holt

134066

POST OFFICE CORNER, c. 1936

Looking towards Cromer Road and showing the new Post Office on the left and the White Lion Hotel which has altered considerably if compared to page 17. The young man to the right of the group on the pavement is Duncan Barrett, who joined the RAF in 1939 and was killed soon after, the only son of Holt's Nurse Barrett.
(A.P. Checkley Collection.)

LING'S GARAGE, CROMER ROAD, c. 1908

Ling's Garage was owned by the Ling brothers. The two open-topped motor-cars in the garage forecourt have been smartly decorated with flowers and ribbons, presumably for a local wedding. The Ling brothers were not only motor engineers, but also the local agents for Siddley Deasey cars. The site is now occupied by the North Norfolk Garage.

(Published by Preston Bros.)

No. 10946

BENGAL LODGE, CROMER ROAD, p.u. 1904

Looking towards Kelling and showing Bengal Lodge which was once the home of Mr. Robert Rust. It was acquired later by Gresham's School for use as a boarding house for some of the younger boys and renamed Kenwyn. At the time of the photograph, the area had not been built up as much as it is today. Notice the unsurfaced road.

CROSSWAYS HOUSE, CROMER ROAD, c. 1908

Photographed near the bend where Pearsons Road joins Cromer Road and showing the rear of Crossways House – nearing completion and being built for Gresham's School. In the foreground a steam traction-engine and drum are threshing a corn stack.

(Published by Preston Bros. – A.P. Checkley collection.)

The Rose Tea Gardens, Cromer Road, Holt

THE ROSE TEA GARDENS, 1929

The Rose Tea Gardens were situated on the Cromer Road, just past the turning to Kelling. They were very popular with visitors during summer months and served afternoon teas outside weather permitting. At the time of the photograph, Mr. Walter G. Stokes was the proprietor and the telephone number was Holt 39. The Gardens closed in the early 1930s to make way for new housing. (This postcard is one of a set of six coloured views.)

22

HOLT HALL, p.u. 1911

Holt Hall is situated between the Cley and Kelling Roads. The hall has beautiful grounds which also contain a large stretch of water. It was built in the Elizabethan style for the Burcham-Rogers family by W.H. Pemberton. It is now owned by the County Council and the building is used by students for courses and seminars.
(Published by A. Clare, Post Office, Market Place, Holt.)

GRESHAM'S SCHOOL, c. 1905

At the turn of the century, the Governors of Gresham's School decided that Gresham's should become a public boarding school. Boarding houses were built along the Cromer Road; the first opening in 1903. The house shown above is called 'Howson's' after the first headmaster. The Assembly Hall, the building with the church-like windows, can be seen in the right background.
(Published by Preston Bros.)

'WOODLANDS', CROMER ROAD, c. 1916

This imposing building was once the home of Mr. Onisiphorous Randall (the name Onisiphorous means 'bringing profit'), a somewhat eccentric gentleman born in Cley in 1798. He made his fortune as a builder in London, but returned to Norfolk and built another wing on to 'Woodlands'. Mr. Randall was also the builder of another house near Salthouse beach called 'Randall's Folly' which was washed away in the 1953 floods that devastated the coastline. Gresham's School bought 'Woodlands' for use as a boarding house for the pupils and it now forms part of the school complex.

HOME PLACE, p.u. 1930

This impressive house, set in its own grounds on the Cromer Road, was built by E. S. Prior in 1905 for the Rev. Percy Lloyd. Apparently, the gentleman's wife took a dislike to the place and would not live there. The building was first called Voewood but it has had several other names: Kelling Place; Home Place, and the City of Leicester Convalescent Home. It was later taken over by the Local Health Authority in 1948.
(Published by Miss E. M. Hall, Stationer, Holt.)

26

FLOOD DAMAGE, HEMPSTEAD ROAD, 1912

The road on the Holt side of Hempstead Mill was washed away to the depth of several feet during the floods which occurred after heavy rain on 26th August, 1912. Mr. Reggie Preston inspects the damage while his sister, Miss Mary Preston (in the white blouse) and Miss Gooch stand in the background. The name of the workman is unknown.
(Published by Preston Bros.)

DONKEY EXPRESS, p.u. 1906

This charming postcard shows a novel form of transport for the two little girls in their smart Edwardian hats and seated in wicker panniers on the donkey's back. According to the correspondence on the reverse of the card, they were the daughters of Mr. Ling, a farmer at Heath Farm, Hempstead Road. Notice that the donkey appears to have three legs! *(Published by Preston Bros.)*

Footpath, near Holt.

THE LOWS, p.u. 1906

The Lows consists of 120 acres of wild heath and woodland to the south of Holt. At one time a racecourse was situated here, near the Norwich Road, and it is recorded that Lord Orford won the Town Plate on his horse 'Ginger' in 1753. Like Spout Hills, the Lows were allotted to the poor in 1810. When the railway was built, cartloads of earth from the excavations were taken to the Lows, and later, during the First World War, a firing range was constructed for training soldiers; now known as Target Hill. Sixty acres of land have now been added to the Lows and the area, which is a haven for wildlife, is managed by the Local Authority, as a Country Park.

HOLT RAILWAY STATION, p.u. 1904

The railway station was situated by Hempstead Road. It was built in 1884 when the railway line was extended from Melton Constable to Holt by the Midland and Great Northern Railway. The building in the picture was seriously damaged by fire in 1927 and rebuilt in 1928. The station buildings were demolished for the construction of the Holt bypass.

Holt Railway Station. J 3529. (*Basham's Series*).

HOLT RAILWAY STATION, c. 1920

A more detailed view of the station buildings. The level-crossing can be seen on the extreme left. The signal-box behind had previously stood near Page and Turner's Granary which stands in the centre background. After the Railway closed the signal box was bought by the "Poppy Line" – The North Norfolk Steam Railway and taken to Weybourne Station by road transport on 4th April, 1966. Unable to negotiate under the Gresham's School Bridge, the vehicle had to reverse all the way back to the Kelling Road turning and take a different route to Weybourne. Part of Page and Turner's granary still stands and now houses the Florida Shoe Factory.

MARKET PLACE, c. 1910

Looking west from Station Road, the old Post Office is shown in the centre of the picture. The shop on its left was Mr. F. S. Ransom's boot and shoe shop, with the top of the Water Tower showing above. To the right of the bushes, out of view, is the School House. During the 1600s, Thomas Cooper, who was master of Gresham's School, was hanged in front of School House for his allegiance to the Royalist cause during the Civil War. The Railway Hotel, left foreground, is rumoured to have a ghost.

FEATHERS HOTEL, HIGH STREET, c. 1924

In the days before planning permission the hotel was ornately decorated with lettering by Holt sign-writer, Arthur Burgess; with flower boxes over the doors, it had a very distinctive appearance. Cattle sales were held in the yard at the rear. The International Stores can be seen on the right of the picture.

(A publicity postcard published by Mr. Cubitt Cooke, proprietor of the Feathers Hotel.)

HIGH STREET, c. 1910

Mr. Harry Culley's distinctive grocery and drapery store can be seen in the left foreground; he also had a shop at Briston. Culley's ceased trading in 1922 and the premises were then taken over by the International Stores. In the right background Lee's Wine Store can be seen with a billboard outside, and to the left, Rounce and Wortley's printing works. No traffic problems in those days!

METHODIST FREE CHURCH. HOLT (*Basham's Series.*) J 1540

METHODIST FREE CHURCH AND HIGH STREET, c. 1916

On the left, the shop belonged to Mr. H. B. Moulton, tailor and outfitter, who also supplied Gresham's School uniforms – including the straw hats. The Methodist Free Church stands in the background. It was designed in the Gothic style and built in 1863, costing around £2,000 and seating four hundred people. On the right, the carrier's cart belonged to Mr. Peck of Edgefield, a flour dealer who made a weekly journey into Holt.
(Printed by Jarrolds for Basham's of Holt.)

BEATING THE BOUNDS, c. 1909

Schoolgirls from the old Church School in Norwich Road dressed for performing the custom of 'Beating the Bounds'; an ancient ritual which involved going round the parish boundaries tapping the hedgerows and earth with sticks. The custom was supposed to ensure the fertility of the soil and a good harvest. May day was believed to be the date for this event.
(Published by Preston Bros.)

HUNWORTH, c. 1913

Hunworth lies in a wooded valley, three-and-a-half miles south of Holt. At the time that this picture was taken, the population was around 190. Today, little has changed in this quiet and peaceful corner of the village. The Glaven still runs over the road, and the cottages, which are now renovated, are still standing. Hunworth is known locally as 'Hunney'.
(A.P. Checkley collection.)

ENTRANCE TO STODY LODGE, c. 1905

Stody Lodge and its famous azalea and water gardens are situated in Stody woods on the road between Briston and Holt. The wooden bungalow pictured here was occupied by Mr. R. Adams, the gardener to Mr. Horsefall, the owner of Stody Lodge at that time. In the 1920s, the bungalow was bought by a Briston baker who dismantled and rebuilt it near the entrance to Plumbs Close, Briston where it still stands. Lord Rothermere had the present Stody Lodge built in the early 1930s.

WEST END, BRISTON, c. 1934

On the left, the grocery and drapery shop belonged to Mr. Sid Reynolds. The shop changed ownership several times before closing and being converted into a private residence. In the background, the house was owned for many years by Mr. Ernie Whittred who ran the local cinema in the Oddfellows Hall for two nights each week. In the right foreground the shop was occupied by Mrs. Cletheroe, general dealer and newsagent.

BRISTON "HORSESHOES", c. 1922

Sidney Maskell was landlord of The Horseshoes when Herbert Remington took this picture of the pub's quoits team. A very popular game at the time, matches were held amongst the local public houses to compete for the Thomas Cooke Cup. The Horsehoes has been renamed and is now known as the John H. Stracey.

THE RUINS OF EDGEFIELD CHURCH, p.u. 1907

The Church of Saint Peter and Saint Paul was pulled down except for the remains pictured here. The new church, nearer the centre of Edgefield, cost around £1,000 to build, and much of the stone from the old church was used in its construction. Canon Hubert Marcon, a much loved and long serving Rector here, was born in Edgefield Rectory in 1850. He succeeded his father in 1876 and served the parish for sixty years.
(A.P. Checkley collection.)

EDGEFIELD, c. 1910

A view of Edgefield, three miles south of Holt, showing the large village pond and Alfred King's blacksmith shop. At this time, the blacksmith was a very important member of the community; mending machinery, making iron-hurdles and shoeing the farmers' horses. At the turn of the century, the population of the village was 477 and this included 14 farmers, so Mr. King must have been kept quite busy!

SALLY AND JIMMY, EDGEFIELD, c. 1920

This quaint old couple, Sally and Jimmy Auger, earned their living on the land, working for local farmers. It is thought they lived in a hut on Edgefield Green. Notice the man's cap under Sally's scarf, her apron made from sacking, and the dangerous-looking reap-hook in her hand. Jimmy's jacket and trousers are tied together with string.

(Published by Herbert Remington of Briston.)

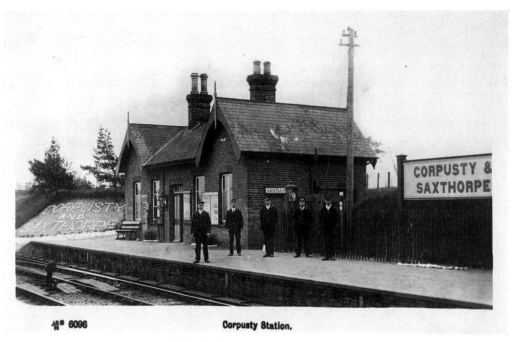

№ 6096   Corpusty Station.

CORPUSTY STATION, c. 1912

The nearest station to Edgefield was Corpusty-with-Saxthorpe. Serving two adjoining villages, it was first stop on the line from Melton Constable to Great Yarmouth. Built in the typical twin-gabled style of the M. & G.N. Railway, the station looks well cared for and the pride and joy of the station-master, Mr. Alfred Sayer, and his staff. Notice the station's name picked out in stones (regularly whitened), on the left of the picture.
(Printed by Jarrolds for Gough's Stores, Corpusty.)

MATLASK, c. 1909

Matlask is a small rural parish six miles south-west of Holt. One of Norfolk's many round-towered churches, St. Peter's has an octagonal belfrey. The chancel collapsed in 1726 and was not rebuilt. When Holt's water-tower was demolished in 1955, the town's water supply was connected to the new well at Matlask. This scene remains almost the same today.
(Published by Preston Bros. – A.P. Checkley collection.)

HEMPSTEAD VILLAGE, c. 1916

A charming rural scene of Hempstead village. The village had two public houses: The White Horse Inn and the Hare and Hounds, both out of view. The little girl with the doll's pram would have gone to Baconsthorpe School, in the adjoining village.

(Printed by Jarrolds for Kemp's Stores and Post Office – A.P. Checkley collection.)

HEMPSTEAD MILL, p.u. 1907

Mr. J. Tuck, who was also a coal-merchant, took over the water-mill from Mr. George Bird, and ran both businesses from these premises. The mill is now a private residence; the wheel remains on the wall, just above the sign board.
(Published by Preston Bros.)

BACONSTHORPE HALL RUINS, c. 1924

Baconsthorpe Hall, or Castle, was originally owned by the Bacon family, from whom the village of Baconsthorpe takes its name. It passed into the hands of the Heydon family in the 15th century until they sold their Norfolk estates in the late 1600s. The Hall, which stands three-quarters-of-a-mile outside the village, was inhabited until one of the turrets collapsed in 1920. The ruins were placed under the guardianship of the Ministry of Works in 1940.

(A.P. Checkley collection.)

BACONSTHORPE, p.u. 1913

Showing the village post office which ran a full postal service, with the Telegraph Office even open for two hours on Sunday mornings! The postmaster was Mr. Frederic Webb, grocer and draper, who was also honorary secretary to the Baconsthorpe Reading Room. The sign on the next house reads "Victorian's Jubilee". It is not clear what these premises were, as only one public house – The Jolly Farmers – is listed in the village. Baconsthorpe is a very ancient parish. St. Mary's Church records were destroyed in a fire at the Rectory in about 1690, with the existing register dating from 1692.

J&S 5043
N

Erpingham Post Office.

ERPINGHAM POST OFFICE, p.u. 1910

This small village post office was run by Mr. Benjamin Barstard who was also a carpenter. Many village post offices were run on similar lines from private houses. However, anyone wishing to send a telegram or a money order had to visit Hanworth Post Office, two miles away. Holt and District was in the Erpingham Rural District Council Catchment area, before coming under North Norfolk Rural District Council.

(Published by Jarrolds for Mr. Barstard.)

Eagle Inn, Erpingham.

THE EAGLE INN, ERPINGHAM, p.u. 1910

Major Dunn was landlord of the Spread Eagle Inn when this picture was taken with some of the customers posing outside.
By 1912 the landlord was Charles Williamson and Major Dunn was listed as a painter and decorator. Notice the rails for
tethering the horses in front of the windows and the old wooden beer barrel in the left foreground – real ale in those days!

KELLING SANATORIUM, p.u. 1911

Kelling was chosen as a site for a sanatorium for the treatment of tuberculosis of the lungs ('Consumption'), because of the purity of the air and proximity to the sea. Standing in thirty-two acres of land, and surrounded by pinewoods, it was opened in 1903 with about fifty beds. Dr. F.W. Burton-Fanning was the Chief Consultant. The postcard shows some of the wards and shelters for open-air treatment. Consumption was rife amongst the population during the early 1900s.
(Published by Preston Bros.)

OPEN-AIR TREATMENT, c. 1909

Patients slept in these chalets, no matter how cold the weather. As can be seen this type had no doors, only curtains, which could be drawn at night. The story is told of nurses sweeping the snow off the bedcovers on winter mornings! Each hut was on a turntable and could be rotated to face any direction. The children's Sanatorium and Bramblewood, for women patients, were built later, and by 1937 there were 170 beds within the complex.

CHILDREN'S SANATORIUM, p.u. 1939

The Children's Sanatorium was built after a public appeal for funds, receiving a large gift of money from Sir Otto Beit, and opening in April 1913 entirely free from debt. Girls from two to sixteen years, and boys from two to thirteen years old were treated here during the early stages of tuberculosis.
(A.P. Checkley collection.)

KELLING MILL, c. 1907

This lovely old post-mill was thought to have stood in Hasgate Lane and to be owned by Mr. James Nurse. It was already falling into disrepair when this picture was taken, and the mill was eventually dismantled in the 1920s. Tragically, one of the workmen, Mr. Gidney, was killed whilst demolishing the brick base.
(Published by Preston Bros.)

SPRINGS HOTEL, WEYBOURNE, p.u. 1907

This impressive hotel was built at the beginning of this century and was situated on the Kelling Road. Even though it had its own nine-hole golf course and the station was close by, the hotel's popularity waned because it was so far from the sea. The building was used, for a time, as a Private Nursing Home for the mentally sick; bars being placed over the windows. Subsidence due to sandy ground caused the building to sink at one end, and after standing empty for some years it was demolished in 1939 as it had become so dangerous.

WEYBOURNE BEACH, c. 1903

These coastguard houses stand at the point where the North Norfolk Coast's cliffs end, and the Saltmarsh coastline, extending through to Hunstanton, begins. When a new Coastguard Station was built, these buildings were then used by civilians, and then became a club for officers from the nearby Army Camp. Considered to be a landmark for the enemy, the buildings were demolished during the early years of World War 2. The wreck of the collier 'Rosalie' lies just offshore, sunk on her maiden voyage in 1914, probably mined or torpedoed by the Germans.
(Published by G.D.J. Spink, Post Office, Weybourne.)

J & S 8324   THE POST OFFICE, LANGHAM.

THE POST OFFICE, LANGHAM, p.u. 1914

Langham village is two miles from the coast and four-and-a-half-miles from Holt. The post office is situated on the corner
of Binham Road. Not a soul in sight except for the baker delivering bread!
(Printed by Jarrold's for Mr. Elijah William Boast, postmaster of Langham – Philip Standley collection.)

"MANOR COTTAGE", LANGHAM, c. 1923

Captain Frederick Marryatt, the famous author of children's books, spent the last few years of his life at Langham in this house. He settled here in 1843 and "The Children of the New Forest" and "The Little Savage" were two of the five books written at Manor Cottage. He suffered indifferent health, and it is said that the news that his eldest son was lost at sea in the "Avenger" so upset him that he died on 2nd August, 1848. A marble tablet to his memory can be seen in Langham Church. Today, there are new houses built near Manor Cottage and Marryatt Close is named after him.

SAXLINGHAM FLOODS, 1912

Many parts of the county suffered as a result of the dreadful flooding on 26th August, 1912. A delivery cart owned by Harry Culley, the Holt draper, overturned due to a large subsidence in the road in the little village of Saxlingham. The population at the time was about 125, and it would appear that the greater part of the male population were eager to be photographed at the scene of the disaster.
(Published by Preston Bros.)

GLANDFORD MILL, c. 1907

Sir Alfred Jodrell, who lived in Bayfield Hall, owned this well maintained water-mill which stands on the River Glaven. Sir Alfred was a great public benefactor who sent a weekly gift of vegetables to the Norfolk and Norwich Hospital, and also chickens and turkeys at Christmas. His main interests were the administration of his estates and the restoration of old churches. The mill is now a private house.
(Published by Preston Bros.)

ST. MARTIN'S CHURCH AND SHELL MUSEUM, GLANDFORD, c. 1930

St. Martin's Church was built during the Middle Ages, and at the turn of the century this little church was in a very dilapidated state. Sir Alfred Jodrell, who had an interest in the restoration of old churches, had it completely rebuilt in memory of his mother, who died in 1896. The Shell Museum, with its Dutch-style gable, stands in the left foreground.

Interior of Shell Museum, Glandford. 145992

GLANDFORD SHELL MUSEUM, c. 1930

Glandford Shell Museum was built in 1915 by Sir Alfred Jodrell. It houses his huge shell collection which was acquired from all parts of the world over many years. Prior to the museum being built, the shells were stored in boxes at Bayfield Hall. Sir Alfred, and his two sisters, Lady Seale and Mrs. Ind, arranged the shells for display.
(A.P. Checkley collection.)

Through the kind permission of
Sir Alfred and Lady Jane Jodrell,

A Bazaar

In Aid of Stody Church,

Will be held **AT BAYFIELD** on the Day of the Grand Fete,

JULY 14TH, 1904,

Under the distinguished patronage of
THE HIGH SHERIFF AND MRS. COLMAN,
THE MARCHIONESS OF LOTHIAN & B. TALBOT, Esq.
THE EARL AND COUNTESS OF ORFORD.
LORD AND LADY HASTINGS.
SIR ALFRED AND LADY JANE JODRELL.
C. W. H. COZENS-HARDY, Esq., MRS. COZENS-HARDY.

The Bazaar will be opened by Mrs. Colman at 3.0 p.m.

Contributions of any kind will be gratefully received by the Stallholders—Mrs. Horsfall, Miss Smith and Mrs. Fullagar.

Conveyances will ply between Holt Station and Bayfield at a moderate charge.

BAYFIELD FÊTE, c. 1904

When the rebuilding of the church at Glandford was almost completed, Sir Alfred Jodrell turned his attention to the restoration of Stody Church. To raise funds, a grand fête was held in the grounds of his home at Bayfield Hall; details of which can be seen on this postcard.
(A.P. Checkley collection.)

BAYFIELD FÊTE, 1904

The main attraction of the Bayfield Fête was the descent of Professor Fleet by parachute from a balloon. Apparently, it took four attempts before he was finally successful.
(Published by Arthur Preston, Holt.)

Parachute Descent by Professor Fleet at Bayfield Fete, July 14th, 1904.

PRINTED AT ARTHUR PRESTON'S "RELIANCE" WORKS, HOLT.

LETHERINGSETT HALL AND CHURCH, c. 1909

William Hardy bought this property in 1780 when it was known as 'Rawlings'. After 1800 it was known as Letheringsett Hall. Numerous alterations have been made over the years, resulting in the elegant building which stands today. The round tower of St. Andrew's Church dates from Norman times, and contains three bells. The church was restored in 1875, and a new porch was built in 1890.

(Published by Preston Bros. – A.P. Checkley collection.)

KING'S HEAD, LETHERINGSETT, c. 1910

The original 'King's Head' was demolished in the early 1800s, when the road nearby was altered. The present inn, pictured here, was constructed of white brick in 1820. The landlord at the time was Mr. Cunningham. The King's Head is now a popular venue for jazz festivals, and is the headquarters of the Holt Lions Club.

(Published by Preston Bros. – A.P. Checkley collection.)

GLAVENSIDE, LETHERINGSETT, c. 1915

Mr. and Mrs. Cozens-Hardy, the owners of 'Glavenside', kindly lent their house to the Red Cross for use as a War Hospital. It opened on 9th December, 1915 with twenty-two beds, plus four extra beds under the verandah which could be used in the summertime for open-air cases.
(Published by Preston Bros. – A.P. Checkley collection.)

BALE STORES, c. 1930

This village store situated on the Field Dalling Road was run by Mrs. Elsie Lake. Her husband, Harry Lake, was a travelling draper. The shop was in the room to the right of the door, and customers were often welcomed by the Pekinese dog pictured in the doorway. The store is now a private residence.
(A.P. Checkley collection.)

No. J. & S. 7875 GUNTHORPE POST OFFICE.

GUNTHORPE POST OFFICE, p.u. 1913

In 1935, under the County Review order, the civil parish of Bale was added to Gunthorpe. Mrs. Margaret Kidd, post-mistress, stands in the doorway of Gunthorpe's Post Office and General Store. One of a row of five cottages, its window has been altered to incorporate the post-box. Notice the advert for Rock Light Lamp Oil over the door. The postman is wearing leather buskins to protect his legs from the cold and wet. The message on the back of the card reads "What a lively old show Gunthorpe is."

THE PRESTON BROTHERS, c. 1909

As so much of Preston Bros. work is shown in this book, it seems appropriate to include this picture of Mr. "Chummy" Preston, seated beside the driver, and Mr. Tom Preston by the rear wheel, with their families on a trip to the coast – believed to be Weybourne. Mr. Ben Empson is the driver of the elegant open-topped carriage. The only sign of the second horse is its two back legs!
(A.P. Checkley collection.)

JUST "A LINE" FROM HOLT, c. 1914

Comic postcards with different designs could be bought and over printed to order with a town's name. Wholesale prices of these cards would be six dozen for 3/3d. (16p).
(Published by E. Mack, Hampstead – A.P. Checkley collection.)